BBC
DOCTOR WHO
Robot of Sherwood

A story based on the original script by
MARK GATISS

Level 2

Retold by Nancy Taylor

Series Editors: Andy Hopkins and Jocelyn Potter

Pearson Education Limited

KAO Two

KAO Park, Harlow,

Essex, CM17 9NA, England

and Associated Companies throughout the world.

ISBN: 978-1-292-20565-6

This edition first published by Pearson Education Ltd 2018

5 7 9 10 8 6

For a complete list of the titles available in the Pearson English Readers series, visit
www.pearsonenglishreaders.com.
Alternatively, write to your local Pearson Education office or
to Pearson English Readers Marketing Department,
Pearson Education, KAO Two, KAO Park, Harlow, Essex, CM17 9NA

Contents

The Doctor

The Doctor comes from Gallifrey, a very long way from Earth, and he is about 2,000 years old. He can move, in his time machine, through space and time. His journeys are exciting, and often dangerous. He helps people – in our world and in other worlds – when he can.

The Doctor never wants to kill anybody. He doesn't use a gun – but he does have a spoon! He uses that in fights. He also has a sonic screwdriver, a very clever machine. It can open doors and see inside things. It can cut things and break things. It can also make explosions. It has many uses in the Doctor's fights for better worlds.

The TARDIS

This time machine looks like a blue police box. In earlier times, British people called the police from these boxes. The TARDIS looks small on the outside but it is very big inside.

The Doctor's Companion: Clara Oswald

The companions are the Doctor's friends and helpers. In this story, his companion is a young English teacher. Clara goes with him to different places in the TARDIS, and helps in his fights. She is very important to him.

Robin Hood

Robin Hood is a hero from children's stories. He takes money from rich people and gives it to poor people. In the stories, he lives in Sherwood Forest with his Merry Men.

The Merry Men

People call them 'merry' because they are usually very happy. They live and work with Robin Hood. The Merry Men fight for a better, happier world for everybody.

The Sheriff of Nottingham

The Sheriff is a bad man. He takes everything from poor people. They also have to work for him or die. He doesn't like Robin Hood and his men because they make his life difficult.

The Sheriff's Knights

The knights work for the Sheriff. They fight for him, and kill for him. They take things from poor people and carry them to the Sheriff's castle. They also have a very important job *inside* the castle...

Introduction

The Doctor turns on his time machine and puts in: Earth. England. Sherwood Forest. About the year 1190. *The machine does its job.*

The Doctor can go anywhere in his time machine, the TARDIS. In this story he moves back in time to the year 1190; the place is Sherwood Forest, near the city of Nottingham. Clara Oswald is the Doctor's companion on the journey, and she is very excited.

They go to Sherwood Forest because Clara wants to meet Robin Hood. When she was a child, she read stories about him. He was one of her heroes. But was Robin Hood a real person – and was he really a hero? Will the Doctor and Clara find him and his friends in the forest? Let's climb into the TARDIS and begin our journey.

You can watch *Doctor Who* on television in Britain and in many other countries. William Hartnell played the First Doctor in 1963 – in black and white! In this story, Peter Capaldi plays the Twelfth Doctor. Jenna Coleman is Clara, his companion.

People watch *Doctor Who* on television because they love the exciting journeys to dangerous places, and the Doctor's clever tricks. They learn about people's lives in earlier times, and see possible futures. Many people follow his journeys for years and years.

A lot of different writers work on the *Doctor Who* stories. Mark Gatiss is the writer of this story and many other stories for film and television. Perhaps you also know his face: he played Mycroft Holmes in *Sherlock* and Tycho Nestoris in *Game of Thrones*.

To Sherwood Forest

'Robin Hood! I want to meet Robin Hood!' shouts Clara.

She and the Doctor are in the TARDIS, the Doctor's time machine and the centre for his planning and thinking.

'Robin Hood? A hero from children's storybooks? We all know the stories. He takes money from rich people and gives it to poor people. But we can only visit *real* people,' the Doctor says.

'But I love those stories. I want to meet him – in the famous Sherwood Forest!' says Clara.

'Robin Hood never lived in Sherwood Forest, Clara. He never lived anywhere! He was only a hero in books,' the Doctor tells his young companion. 'Your hero's not real.'

'But *you're* real,' Clara says.

'Excuse me?' The Doctor doesn't understand.

'Well, you help people every minute of every day. You're a hero, too, and I like heroes,' says Clara.

The Doctor smiles. 'I have to do *something* with my time.' He tries again. 'Clara, think of a *real* hero and a *real* place. Don't you want to meet Gandhi or Winston Churchill? They were very interesting. Or we could go to China, or Mars.'

'No, please try to find Robin Hood,' Clara says again.

'Well, I'll try,' the Doctor says. 'Please remember: the TARDIS goes to *real* places, in *real* times.'

The Doctor turns on his time machine and puts in: *Earth. England. Sherwood Forest. About the year 1190.* The machine does its job.

Suddenly the TARDIS is sitting in a sunny green forest, next to a small river. The Doctor looks outside.

'Hmm. I can see a small river with a bridge across it,' he tells Clara. 'But I can't see any pretty castles, happy villagers or strong knights. And I can't see the famous Robin Hood. I told you. He's not real.'

An arrow hits the TARDIS and the Doctor jumps. A man comes out

An arrow hits the Tardis and the Doctor jumps.

from behind a tree with a bow in his hand. He is wearing green clothes from head to foot.

'Are you looking for Robin Hood? That's me!' shouts the man.

'Ha-ha-ha! That was a good trick with your box, sir. How did you do it?'

'No trick! You're looking at the TARDIS,' says the Doctor.

'Hmm. Its name isn't important, old man, and now it's mine,' cries Robin. 'I take things from people like you.'

'And I feel sorry for people like *you*,' answers the Doctor.

'But today I'll take your box. Ha-ha-ha!' laughs Robin.

'Why do you laugh so much? Don't people get angry when you laugh all the time?' the Doctor asks. He doesn't like the young man.

'Perhaps they do,' Robin says. He thinks about it for a minute. But he forgets about the question when the door to the TARDIS suddenly opens. 'Excuse me! What's this?' he asks the Doctor.

Clara is coming out of the TARDIS. She is wearing a beautiful red dress from an earlier age, perhaps from about 1190.

'Are there any more young women in there?' Robin asks.

'Doctor!' shouts Clara. 'You found him!'

'That is *not* Robin Hood,' the Doctor says. 'Robin

Hood is *not* real.'

'Not real?' shouts Robin. 'But I'm going to fight you for your box. *That's* real!'

'Nobody can take the TARDIS!' the Doctor shouts.

'Well, I'll try,' Robin says. He pulls out his sword. 'Where's your sword, old man?'

The Doctor takes a spoon from inside his jacket. He always has his spoon with him. He uses it when he fights. He usually wins his fights because he is cleverer than people with guns or swords.

'I can win without a sword because I'm the Doctor,' he answers. 'Are you ready? Let's fight!'

The Doctor hits Robin on the back of his head with his spoon.

'Doctor, you're wonderful!' shouts Clara.

'This isn't my first fight, Clara. And, remember, he isn't real,' the Doctor tells his young companion.

Then Robin runs to the Doctor and cuts the older man's jacket with his sword. The Doctor is angry now. With his arms above his head, he turns quickly. He is now back to back with Robin, and with a quick push he sends the younger man into the river.

'You see, Clara. It's *my* box. *My* TARDIS,' the Doctor says.

'But where's Robin Hood?' Clara asks unhappily.

She and the Doctor look into the water, but they can't see anybody or anything. Then suddenly Robin is behind them and pushes the Doctor into the water. He and Clara look down at the wet, angry Doctor and laugh.

'Ha-ha-ha!'

'A little water won't hurt you or me,' says Robin Hood to the Doctor when the Doctor is on dry ground again. The Doctor is wet from head to foot. 'This is an exciting day for me. Two new friends! A doctor and, of course, his lovely companion.'

They walk through the trees and come to a pretty place in the forest. A number of men are sitting or standing there.

'Are we *really* in Sherwood Forest?' Clara asks Robin. 'Does the Sheriff of Nottingham live near here, too?'

'Yes, he does,' answers Robin. 'I live here in the forest, and the Sheriff lives in a big castle. But now you have to meet my men. We're like brothers. When I fight, they fight with me.'

'And we take from rich people when we can,' says Will Scarlett.

'Yes. Ha-ha-ha!' laughs Robin. 'That's Will. He's good with a sword and fast with a smile. And there's Friar Tuck, the man with the big stomach. He loves food more than anything. Alan-a-Dale plays music and sings for us. And last is my greatest – and largest – friend: Little John.'

'Oh, this is wonderful!' cries Clara. 'You really *are* Robin Hood and his Merry Men.'

'That's a good name for us! We're the Merry Men! Ha-ha-ha! But these are sad days for us,' says Robin.

'Please! Stop laughing! Are you all stupid?' shouts the Doctor.

He is walking round the Merry Men. He carefully looks at each man. They *look* real. He feels Little John's arm. It *feels* real. He pulls a hair out of Will Scarlett's head. That's real, too. The Doctor doesn't understand. He knows that they *can't* be real. What trick is this?

'Your friend is strange. Why is he looking at us like that? Why is he interested in our hair?' Robin asks Clara. 'Is he really from this world?'

'Well, no, most of the time he isn't. But forget about the Doctor. Why are these sad days for you and your men?' asks Clara.

Alan-a-Dale hears Clara and Robin's conversation and begins to sing:

'This forest today is sad

Because our Sheriff is bad.

And so we will fight

All day and all night.'

'Be quiet, please, Alan,' says Robin. He turns to Clara again. 'I'll tell you some of our story. In the past, we worked hard but we had happy lives. Then the Sheriff of Nottingham arrived. He takes everything, and now our people are poor and hungry. They have to work for him or die. Before the Sheriff came here, I was rich. I lived in a castle. My name was—'

'Robert of Loxley,' Clara says happily. She remembers the stories well.

'But now you have to meet my men. We're like brothers. When I fight, they fight with me.'

Robin looks at her. 'Yes, how did you know? I was an important man in Nottingham. But the Sheriff and I had different ideas. He took everything from me, and I lost the most important person in my life. Now my men and I fight the Sheriff every day.'

'Who was that important person? Was her name Marian?' asks Clara.

'What?' Robin asks. 'You're very clever. Do you know her?'

'I think I remember her,' Clara says.

'Marian wanted me to fight, but I was afraid. Now the forest's my castle and the ground's my bed. I'll find my love one day, after my last fight with the Sheriff.'

The Doctor isn't listening. He is looking at the sun. He turns to Robin.

'What time of the year is it, Mr Hood?' he asks.

'The month is October, so we're in the autumn,' Robin tells him.

'Autumn?' says the Doctor. 'But the trees are green and the sun's high in the sky. Does it feel like autumn to you, Clara?'

'Perhaps autumn was different in 1190,' says Clara.

'Please excuse me,' says Robin. 'We have to get ready for a contest tomorrow at the Sheriff's castle. The best bowman will win a gold arrow.'

'But it's a trick!' shouts Clara. She knows that story, too. 'You can't go!'

'We know that it's a trick. But I'm the best bowman in England. I'm going to win that arrow. Ha-ha-ha!'

The Merry Men laugh with Robin.

'Please stop laughing! It hurts my head, and that wasn't funny,' says the Doctor. He turns to Clara and says quietly, 'Remember, he's not real.'

'But he's a hero,' answers Clara.

'Only in storybooks,' the Doctor says. 'Why do you think that there are *real* heroes?'

Clara looks into his eyes. 'Don't you know?' she answers with a smile.

The Contest

Outside a small house near Sherwood Forest, an old man and a young woman look afraid. Two of the Sheriff's knights are shouting at them. They are pulling the young woman away from the old man. They want to take her back to the Sheriff's castle.

'Please stop!' shouts the old man at the knights. 'Take my money. Take my house. But please, don't take this dear child. She's everything to me.'

'Don't cry, Mr Quayle. Everything will be all right,' says the young woman.

But it isn't all right. The knights pull her away from the old man.

'Why are you doing the Sheriff's dirty work?' Mr Quayle shouts at the knights. 'Where is he? I'll kill him with my two hands.'

'Oh, really?' says one of the knights. 'An old man like you will kill the sheriff? Well, now you can try. Here he is.'

The Sheriff of Nottingham gets off his horse and walks to the house. He looks at the old man and the young woman.

'Are you from Nottingham?' the Sheriff asks the young woman. 'Do I know you?'

'She's visiting me!' shouts Mr Quayle. 'Don't hurt her!'

'I'm new here, sir,' answers the woman. 'Mr Quayle is the kindest man.

He gave me food and a bed when I lost my home.'

'You look strong,' the Sheriff says. 'Take her to my castle,' he tells his knights. 'We can use her in the kitchens.'

'And the old man?' asks a knight.

'We can't use *him*. It's the sword for him,' says the Sheriff, and he kills the old man.

'No!' cries the young woman.

But old Mr Quayle is dead, and the knights take her to the castle.

The next afternoon, people from towns and villages near Nottingham arrive at the Sheriff's castle for the contest for the gold arrow. Everybody enjoys the exciting day.

Near the end of the contest, the fight is between the two best bowmen: the Sheriff of Nottingham and Robin Hood.

'I think that we can make this contest more interesting,' Robin says to the Sheriff.

'Interesting? In what way?' asks the Sheriff.

'The target is very near us. Let's move it back twenty metres. Do you think you can hit it then?' Robin asks.

'Why not? Move the target!' the Sheriff shouts at his knights.

'Ready, bowmen?' shouts a knight.

'Watch me!' the Sheriff answers.

The Sheriff's arrow hits the centre of the target.

Then Robin's arrow hits the centre of the Sheriff's arrow. It cuts the Sheriff's arrow into two halves. The gold arrow is Robin's.

But wait! There is a third bowman, the Doctor, and his arrow cuts *Robin's* arrow in two.

The Sheriff takes out another arrow, but the Doctor has a new plan. Before the Sheriff's arrow is ready, the Doctor uses his sonic screwdriver. The target explodes.

'What happened?' the Sheriff shouts angrily. 'What trick was that? Knights! Bring that thing to me.' He wants to see the sonic screwdriver.

The target explodes.

'Take those three people to the dungeon.'

But before the Sheriff's knights get to Robin, Robin turns to the Doctor.

'Let's fight,' he says quietly. 'I'll help you, Doctor.'

'I don't want your help. I want to know more about this Sheriff,' the Doctor says.

'Not now! Now it's time for a fight. And I am Robin Hood!'

Robin quickly takes his sword out and cuts off one of the knight's arms. Everybody goes quiet. They look at the thing on the ground. It isn't a real arm. Inside, it looks like a small machine. It's *not* the arm of a real man!

'Ha! Robots! I was right!' cries the Doctor. 'The knights aren't real men. There are machines under their hats and inside their clothes. Nothing here is real!'

'Kill that man! Kill all of them!' shouts the Sheriff to the robot-knights.

'No, don't kill us. We don't want to fight,' the Doctor tells the Sheriff. 'Mr Hood, put down your sword!'

'What are you talking about?' cries Robin. 'Of *course* we want to fight!'

'No, *I* don't want to fight,' the Doctor says. He speaks quietly to Robin.

'No, I don't want to fight,' the Doctor says. He speaks quietly to Robin. 'I have to learn more about the Sheriff and these robots.'

'I have to learn more about the Sheriff and these robots. We can do that from *inside* the castle.' He turns to the Sheriff. 'And Mr Hood and his Merry Men are going to stop now, too.'

'Really?' says the Sheriff. He doesn't understand. Is this a trick? 'Take them to the dungeon!' the Sheriff shouts again at his robot-knights.

'Run, men, run!' cries Robin to his Merry Men. 'Live and fight another day!'

The Merry Men leave quickly and run back to the forest.

The robot-knights push the Doctor, Robin Hood and Clara down the stairs and into a small room in the dungeon below the castle.

When the robot-knights leave, Robin says, 'Why did you do that? We could win that fight.'

'We couldn't win. Remember, the Sheriff took my sonic screwdriver,' the Doctor says. 'And we can learn more about his plans in here.'

'Really? Well, we're here now,' Robin says, 'so we have to have a plan. And it has to be better than the Sheriff's plan for *us*.'

'Good idea,' says Clara. 'Doctor, do you have a plan?'

'I *always* have a plan,' says the Doctor.

'Me too,' says Robin. '*I* always have a plan, too.'

'Well, Robin, what's *your* plan?' asks Clara.

'I'm thinking. I'll tell you in a minute,' Robin says.

'And you, Doctor? Do you *really* have a plan? A plan without a sonic screwdriver?' Clara asks.

'Quiet! I'm thinking, too,' the Doctor says. 'And my plan will be better than his!'

'Never! Your last plan put us in this dungeon. Was that a great plan? Ha-ha-ha!' laughs Robin.

'Oh, please stop laughing or kill me now,' says the Doctor.

'But you're funny, old grey man. And I think I'm going to laugh again. Ha-ha-ha!'

'Clara, stop him or kill me!' cries the Doctor.

'Two stupid men! Stop fighting and think!' Clara shouts.

The three people in the dungeon stop talking. They are trying to think of a plan.

After many dark, quiet hours, the dungeon door suddenly opens and an ugly little man walks in.

'The Sheriff wants to talk to the boss. Which of you is that?' asks the little man.

'I can trick the Sheriff easily and get us out of here,' the Doctor says to Robin and Clara. 'You know that *I'm* the boss.'

'No, no,' Robin says. 'I understand the Sheriff better. I'll fight him with my two hands and kick him with my feet.'

'Please be quiet and think!' shouts Clara. 'Perhaps the Sheriff wants to *talk*, not fight.'

'You're right, madam. Come with me. You're the most intelligent person here.' The little man looks at the Doctor and Robin and says, 'You know, she's *very* clever.'

For a minute or two, the Doctor and Robin can't speak.

The Sheriff's Plan

Earlier that afternoon there was a lot of fire and noise at the Sheriff's castle when the target exploded. Friar Tuck looked round. Nobody saw him when he took the gold arrow. He quickly put it under his clothes and ran back to Sherwood Forest with the other Merry Men.

Now the Merry Men are sitting next to their big fire, and looking at the arrow.

'It's a beautiful thing,' says Little John.

'Yes,' says Will Scarlett. 'We can sell it and use the money for food for our families and friends. We can all eat well for a year or more.'

'But tonight we'll sleep. Then we can help Robin in the morning,' Little John says.

'Isn't there something strange about the Sheriff?' asks Alan-a-Dale.

'What's that?' Little John asks.

'He has everything, but he always wants more gold. What does he *do* with his bags of gold?'

The Sheriff and Clara are having dinner at a long table in the beautiful dining-room of the castle. There is very good food from many different countries on the table.

'Eat, madam, eat! Enjoy this wonderful food. Aren't you hungry?' the Sheriff asks. 'Drink this wine. It's very expensive, you know. Aren't you thirsty?'

'No, thank you. I had a cup of coffee and a small box of chocolates this morning,' Clara tells him.

'Your words are strange to me,' the Sheriff says. 'What are chocolates? And coffee?'

'They're from *my* world, not yours,' says Clara.

'Yes,' says Will Scarlett. 'We can sell it and use the money for food for our families and friends. We can all eat well for a year or more.'

'I like you, madam. You're … different. And these things from your friend's jacket are different, too.' The Sheriff looks at the Doctor's sandwiches, his famous spoon and the sonic screwdriver. He shows Clara the screwdriver and says, 'Tell me. What can this thing do? Is it dangerous? Are you and your friend really from another world?'

'*You're* the person with the robot-knights. Where are *they* from?' asks Clara.

'The knights are important to *me*, not to you. Forget about them.'

The Sheriff and his robot-knights go round Nottingham and the villages every day. They take things from poor people and bring everything back to the castle.

'More beautiful gold plates!' the Sheriff says happily. 'Put the best ones in the dungeon. I'll use them in my dining room.'

'And the other things?' one of the robot-knights asks.

'Put all of them in the big room with the large bath. The gold things are the most important. Be careful with them,' the Sheriff says.

The robot-knights take the good gold plates to the dungeon. Then they carry the other things to the room with the bath.

On the right, there is a small mountain of gold. Other things are on the left. Every evening the robot-knights light a big fire under the very large bath. Then they throw the gold into the bath. Slowly, it turns into a sea of hot gold.

Why does the Sheriff want this gold? The robot-knights don't know. They only know that the Sheriff is their boss now. They have to do their job.

In the dining-room, the Sheriff's conversation with Clara changes.

'Talk to me about more interesting things,' he says. 'Beautiful things … lovely ideas.'

'Oh, yes!' Clara says. 'I've got a problem and only a great, intelligent man can help me with it. I'd like to discuss it with you – and only with you. Last week I saw some strange lights in the night sky.'

'You saw them, too?' asks the Sheriff. Now he is interested.

'Yes! Lights and strange men. But I didn't tell anybody. Do *you* know anything about them? Did you speak to the strange men?' Clara questions the Sheriff carefully.

'Yes, I did. I'll tell you, but first tell me *your* story. What did you learn about those strange men?' the Sheriff asks.

'Oh, no, no. You have to speak first,' Clara says.

'But why?' asks the Sheriff.

'Because you're a great man. I'm only a poor, weak girl. A strong, clever man always speaks first. Please, tell me your story.'

'Of course, you're right. I *do* always speak first,' the Sheriff says. 'Well, think of a strong, intelligent man – tall and rich, and really wonderful in every way. Do you have a picture of that man in your head?'

'Oh, yes! I can see him, I think!' Clara says cleverly. 'Is he an important man?'

'Yes! But nobody likes him. I don't know why. The people of Nottingham don't listen to him. They're very stupid, and they don't understand him or his great plans,' the Sheriff tells Clara.

'The skyship was the most beautiful thing in the world. Its lights were very strong, but also really lovely. And then suddenly the skyship fell to the ground.'

'Did the lights in the sky change everything for … that man?' Clara asks quietly.

'The skyship was the most beautiful thing in the world. Its lights were very strong, but also really lovely. And then suddenly the skyship fell to the ground. I – he – could see a lot of fire and smoke,' the Sheriff begins.

'I remember that!' Clara cries. 'What did the great man do?'

'He – of course it was me – talked to the men in the skyship. They weren't people. They were robots! They told me everything about the skyship. And now I'm their boss. With the robots and their skyship, I'll have the world at my feet. I'll start with Nottingham. Then tomorrow, Derby.'

'And then?' asks Clara.

'Then, Lincoln and … London!'

'Don't stop there!' Clara says. She is laughing at him now. 'You have a skyship – we call it a spaceship – and robots. You can have the world by next weekend.'

'Stop!' shouts the Sheriff. 'I'll make my plans without your help. Now, I'm interested in *your* story. Begin!'

'Oh, but I don't have one,' Clara says.

'What? Was it a trick?' asks the Sheriff.

'Yes, I'm clever, too. I know that men like to tell their stories.'

'You *are* clever. *Very* clever. I can use you,' the Sheriff says.

'For what?' Clara asks. She is not happy with the conversation now.

'Every man has to have a great woman next to him.'

He tries to pull Clara to him, but she pushes him away.

'You won't find your great woman here,' Clara tells the Sheriff. 'Don't come near me again, or you'll be sorry.'

The Spaceship

In the dungeon, Robin Hood and the Doctor have to think of a plan. How can they help Clara?

'*I* know!' says Robin suddenly. 'Shout for that little man! Tell him that you're really, really ill.'

'It's *your* plan,' says the Doctor coldly. '*You* shout.'

'No, no. That won't work,' says Robin.

'Why?'

'Because you're old and you *look* ill. You're as white as milk. Don't you eat any vegetables?' asks Robin.

'I'm not going to shout. *You* shout.'

'All right. All right. Tell him that I'm very ill. Help! Help!' shouts Robin very loudly. 'Help, please, help us. I'm dying.'

The ugly little man comes to the door of the dungeon.

'What's that noise?' he asks.

'My friend's very ill,' the Doctor tells the little man. 'He always feels ill when he's afraid. He has to have clean water and hot food. Without those, he'll die. He's getting weaker every minute.'

'He can die today or I can kill him tomorrow. Let's think about it,' says the little man. He doesn't speak for a minute. Then he says, 'Today's better.'

'And what will happen to the money?' asks the Doctor.

'Money?' asks the little man. Now he is interested.

'Oh, sorry! I forgot about that,' the Doctor says.

'Tell me about it. Then perhaps I'll help your friend,' says the little man.

'Robin Hood carries a note from a very important Englishman,' the Doctor tells him. He says a name, quietly, and the little man's eyes open wide. 'He'll pay a lot of money for help with his plans.'

'Is it *really* a lot of money? What do I have to do?' asks the little man.

'Come nearer, come nearer. This is for your ears only,' the Doctor tells him.

The little man goes into the dungeon and moves next to the Doctor. Robin stands up and runs behind the man. Then he hits the ugly little man on the head with a chair.

'Quick!' says the Doctor. 'Let's get out of here and close the door. Now *he's* the man in the dungeon.'

Robin Hood and the Doctor leave the dungeon quietly and move from room to room in the dark castle. They are looking for Clara, but suddenly they find something strange and wonderful.

'Look at this!' shouts the Doctor.

'I don't understand,' Robin says. 'What *is* this?'

'It's a spaceship, from the future. It's from about the year 2900, and it's real! Look at these computers and machines. This is very exciting,' the Doctor tells Robin.

'I don't understand anything!' Robin says.

The Doctor tries again. 'It's a spaceship. It came down from space – from a long, long way away – and it stopped *inside* the castle. It's on its way to somewhere.'

The Doctor looks carefully at the computers. 'Look at this map. You can see the name of a place: The Promised Land. The spaceship wants to go there, but ...'

He looks at the other machines. 'Yes, there's a problem with the spaceship. It isn't working. Radiation is leaving the ship and getting into the sky above Nottingham. It can't fly – and now I understand the warm weather here.'

'What *are* you talking about?' asks Robin.

'Remember, I told you earlier. Autumn isn't usually as hot and as green as this. The radiation from the spaceship is changing the weather. And look at this.'

He shows Robin something on one of the computers. The younger man looks at picture after picture from famous storybooks and films.

'What am I looking at?' asks Robin. He doesn't know anything about books or films.

'Each of these shows the name of a story. Look! Many of the stories are about Robin Hood.'

'Why am *I* there?' Robin asks. Suddenly he is interested.

'Because the robots want to *use* your story. They know that people love heroes. Poor people hope that heroes can change their sad lives,' the Doctor tells Robin. 'The stories make them happier.

'You and the Sheriff of Nottingham are here on Earth because the robots *put* you here. The people of Nottingham want a hero, and you're it. You give them hope for a better life in the future. They work for the Sheriff and his robot-knights today because you'll give that happy future to them one day.'

'But I don't *come* from a story!' shouts Robin.

'Don't you? What are you *really*? Please tell me,' the Doctor asks.

'What do you mean?' Robin asks.

'You're a robot, too. You're not real and you know it! Look at your beautiful eyes and your wonderful white teeth and your clean hair. Nobody in Nottingham in 1190 was as well and as strong as you. Tell me your robot name,' the Doctor says.

'Do you think that I work with the Sheriff of Nottingham and some strange knights from the sky?' asks Robin.

'Sorry, but I do,' the Doctor tells him.

'You dog!' shouts Robin. 'How can you think that about me? Why didn't I kill you at the river?'

Suddenly the door behind the Doctor and Robin Hood explodes. A robot-knight walks through the smoke with the Sheriff and Clara.

'Clara!' cries the Doctor. 'Are you all right?'

'Be quiet, old man!' shouts the Sheriff. Then he turns to the robot-knight and says, 'Kill him! And kill Robin Hood!'

'Oh, stop this. We're not in a theatre,' the Doctor says.

'Doctor, what are you talking about?' asks Clara.

'Clara, can't you see? The Sheriff and your Robin Hood aren't real. The robot-knights can't kill people from storybooks,' the Doctor tells Clara.

'No! Stop them! They really *are* going to kill Robin,' shouts Clara. 'Doctor, do something!'

'Sheriff, stop playing tricks. I know that you're not real,' the Doctor says.

Suddenly there is another explosion. Clara quickly stands between Robin and the dangerous fire and smoke. But he moves behind her and pulls her away from the smoke to the window.

'What are you doing, Robin?' Clara asks.

'We're going to live – not die!' shouts Robin.

His back is to the open window. With his arms round Clara, he jumps into the dark night. *SPLASH!* The two young people hit the water below the castle. The Doctor and the Sheriff look down, but they can only see the water and, above it, the black sky.

'I'm sorry about the girl,' the Sheriff says sadly. 'She was a possible wife for me: pretty, clever and strong. But she and Robin Hood were dangerous. They had to go – one way or another. Goodbye to them!'

The Doctor isn't listening to the Sheriff. He is looking out of the window. He can see Clara and Robin on the ground opposite the castle. And now Robin is carrying Clara away.

The Fight in the Dungeon

Robin Hood carries Clara through the dark forest. She is sleeping when he puts her down carefully on the ground. She is cold and wet, but will get warm and dry near the Merry Men's big fire.

Robin and his men watch her.

'Isn't she lovely?' Robin says.

'Yes, you're right, Robin,' Little John says. 'She's beautiful.'

Then they see a little smile on Clara's face, and suddenly she opens one eye.

'Clara! Are you OK?' Robin shouts.

'Of course I am!' she answers, and sits up. 'I like being here with you and your Merry Men. And you think that I'm lovely. How nice! But what happened to the Doctor? Is he OK?'

'I'm sorry, Clara. We don't know,' Robin tells her. 'And we don't know anything about the man. Is he dangerous?'

'No, no, no!' Clara shouts. 'He's a good person. A great man. He's the best!'

'But he thinks that I'm not real! Is *he* real?' asks Robin.

'In many ways, he's the same as you,' Clara tells Robin. 'But *nobody* knows everything about the Doctor.'

'Hmm. Where does he live?' asks Robin.

'Sometimes he lives in London, in the TARDIS,' answers Clara.

'That box?' Robin says. 'Isn't it small for a house?'

'Outside it looks small, but inside it's very big. There are a lot of rooms. It's also the Doctor's time machine and the centre for his thinking and planning,' says Clara.

'And his age? How old is he?' Little John asks.

'Nobody can answer that,' Clara tells them. 'Sometimes he's old, and sometimes he's young. He can move into the future or go back into the past. The Doctor isn't from our world. He can move from one world into another in his TARDIS.'

'How does he do that?' Little John asks.

'I don't know. I'm only his companion and helper. I learn new things about him every day,' Clara answers. 'He's one of my heroes.'

'Why?' Will Scarlett asks.

She is sleeping when he puts her down carefully on the ground. She is cold and wet, but will get warm and dry near the Merry Men's big fire.

'When he was young, he wanted to do good things. So one night he took the TARDIS and began this life. He wants to make the world better. He likes to help poor, ill, hungry, old or weak people. He's kind to everybody – on Earth, in this world, and in other worlds out there.' Clara looks up at the sky, into space. 'Do you like him better now?' she asks Robin.

'Robin! You *have* to like him. He's Robin Hood from a different world,' says Friar Tuck.

The other Merry Men laugh with Friar Tuck: 'Ha-ha-ha!'

'That's right!' cries Clara. 'Robin Hood and the Doctor are great men! My two heroes!'

At the same time, the Doctor is face to face with the Sheriff.

'You can't win this fight – you and your clever robots. I understand your plan,' he says.

'Oh, you think that you know my plans?' the Sheriff asks.

'You and your robots are taking everything from the people of Nottingham,' the Doctor says. But then he stops and thinks for a minute. 'It's gold! Gold! Of course! Gold! You have to repair the spaceship and you can use gold for that. The spaceship won't fly again without it.'

'I have the gold and my plan will work,' the Sheriff says. 'We'll leave in the skyship today or tomorrow. Wait and see.'

'Where do you want to go?' the Doctor asks.

'To London! All of England will be mine,' the Sheriff answers. 'And then, the world!'

'The spaceship is 48% ready. It will be 100% ready in twenty-four hours.' These words come from one of the robot-knights. He is sitting at a computer. The numbers in front of him are slowly going up.

'You're wrong,' the Doctor says. 'I know about spaceships. It won't work. This ship can't fly.'

'Look over there,' the Sheriff tells the Doctor.

The Doctor turns, and a robot-knight hits him on the head with a sword.

The Doctor wakes up in the Sheriff's dungeon again. This time, his companions are many of the poor people of Nottingham.

'Why am I in this dirty dungeon again?' the Doctor says to the walls. 'I have to stop that stupid Sheriff and his robot-knights. They don't understand the machines inside the spaceship. Dangerous radiation is coming out of it and it isn't working well. What are they thinking? Yes, perhaps it can climb a *little* way into the sky, but then it will explode. Oh, that stupid, stupid Sheriff!'

Suddenly he sees a young woman. She is the woman from Mr Quayle's little house near Sherwood Forest.

'What are you looking at?' the Doctor asks. 'Who are you?'

'I'm nobody, but I heard your last words. Did you say something about the stupid Sheriff?' she asks quietly.

'Yes,' the Doctor says. 'He's stupid and very dangerous. And possibly, he's a robot.'

'What's a robot?' asks the young woman. 'I don't understand. But I know that the Sheriff's doing something with gold. Look round this dungeon. There are gold plates on every shelf and in those boxes and bags next to the wall. What can that mean?'

'There's a spaceship in this castle. It fell back to Earth from the future, from another … well, from the sky. With the gold, the Sheriff can repair the spaceship. He thinks that the spaceship will fly as well as before. But he's wrong! When it explodes above Nottingham, it will kill half of the people in England. Do you understand?'

'I think that I do. So the gold is important for his plan. Can we stop him?' the young woman asks.

'We can try. Here's my idea. We have to make a lot of noise. Tell everybody in the dungeon. Now!'

Everybody starts to shout and hit the walls.

One of the robot-knights throws open the door of the dungeon and walks in. He looks at the Doctor and his new companion and shouts, 'Quiet, everybody! You two are the problem. Follow me!'

'Sorry. We have a *different* idea,' the Doctor answers.

The robot-knight takes out his laser gun and the fight begins. He tries to hit the Doctor, but the Doctor has one of the gold plates in his hands. The young woman has one of the plates, too. Everybody in the dungeon is using one. When the robot tries to hit somebody with his gun, the laser hits a gold plate. Then it flies back at the robot. When the laser hits him, the robot explodes.

More robots hear the noise and run into the dungeon. But the Doctor and his new companions are ready for them. They stop the lasers with the gold plates. When the lasers fly back at the robots, they kill the robots one after another.

'Look, everybody! Here's the last robot. Get ready!' the Doctor shouts.

Everybody is ready with their gold plates. This last robot tries to hit somebody with his laser gun. The laser flies round the dungeon and hits one gold plate, and then the next. And the next and the next. When the laser gets back to the robot, he explodes.

'You're wonderful!' the young woman shouts at the Doctor. 'You're our hero!'

'Yes, we won that fight,' the Doctor says. 'But now we have to get out of here. Out, out, out! Everybody get out. Quickly!

More robots hear the noise and run into the dungeon. But the Doctor and his new companions are ready for them.

The End of the Sheriff

At the same time as the fight in the dungeon, the Sheriff of Nottingham is in the spaceship. He is studying a map of the world on a computer. He puts his finger on one country after another and repeats, 'Mine. Mine. Mine.'

He hears a robot-knight behind him say, 'The spaceship is 75% ready.'

Another computer shows Robin and Clara in the forest with the Merry Men.

'What's this?' he shouts. 'Those two aren't dead!' He turns to his robot-knights and says, 'We have to kill them today.'

Then the Sheriff looks at a different computer. On that computer, he can see the Doctor and his companions in the dungeon. They are fighting the robot-knights – and winning.

'You think that you're very clever, Doctor,' the Sheriff thinks. 'But do you really think that you and some unimportant little villagers can stop *me*?'

He hears the robot-knight behind him again: 'The spaceship is 82% ready.'

The Sheriff looks at the computer in front of him and thinks hard. 'How can I kill that difficult Doctor?' he thinks. 'My job is more difficult with him in my way.'

On the computer, the Sheriff sees the explosion of the last robot-knight.

Suddenly the door to the spaceship opens and the Doctor walks in.

The Sheriff turns to him and says, 'Perhaps you're dangerous, Doctor.

But you and your villagers can't stop me. Not today! Never!'

'You're funny today, Sheriff, but I won't laugh at you,' the Doctor answers. 'The important thing is this: you can't use gold for all the repairs to the spaceship. There will always be problems. The spaceship will climb into the sky, but then it will explode. Half of the people in England will die. Your plan won't work because there won't be an England.'

'You don't know anything. I *will* have my skyship, and I *will* have all of England!' the Sheriff cries. 'That's my great plan!'

More robot-knights come into the spaceship through the door behind the Doctor.

'Listen to me,' the Doctor says to the Sheriff. 'Give Clara to me, and I'll help you.'

'Clara isn't here. She's with your friend, Robin Hood,' the Sheriff tells the Doctor. 'Don't you remember? She jumped out of the castle with him.'

'My friend? No! Robin Hood isn't my friend. He's one of your robots!' shouts the Doctor.

'Robin Hood and I aren't friends,' the Sheriff says. 'I plan to kill him this afternoon. I'm going to enjoy that.'

'You won't kill him. He's as important to you as those robot-knights,' the Doctor says. 'You can tell me.'

'How is Robin Hood important to me?' asks the Sheriff.

'He gives hope to the people of Nottingham. They think that he'll fight for them,' the Doctor tells the Sheriff.

'Yes – and now you know that he's not my friend. How *can* he be? He's different from me in every way. Robin Hood – my friend? That's a stupid idea,' laughs the Sheriff.

'You're right.' The Doctor stops and thinks. 'Robin Hood isn't real,' he repeats. 'He's a hero, yes, but only in children's stories.'

Robin Hood arrives in the castle and hears the Doctor's words.

'Thank you!' he shouts. 'I *am* that hero, and I'm here with a real friend.'

The Doctor and the Sheriff walk out of the spaceship and see Clara and

Robin at the top of the stairs. Robin puts his arms round Clara and jumps to the floor below, with her in his arms.

The Doctor smiles happily at Clara.

'Are you all right?' he asks his young companion.

'Me? Of course! Never better! Life with Robin is very exciting!'

'Good,' the Doctor answers. 'But we haven't got a lot of time now. The castle is going to explode in minutes. Let's plan.'

But Robin isn't listening to the Doctor. He looks at the Sheriff and says, 'My Merry Men are here, in the castle. After today, the castle will be mine. Are you ready for the biggest fight of your life?'

'I'm always ready,' cries the Sheriff. The robot-knights want to help him, but he stops them. 'This fight is between me and Robin Hood. I can win without your tricks. What do you say, young hero? Do you want to die?'

Robin and the Sheriff begin their fight. The Sheriff hits Robin with his sword and laughs.

'Ha-ha-ha! Today you're going to lose your most important fight. Then you'll have to follow me or die.'

'But I can't die today. I enjoy playing games with you. I don't want to stop that. Ha-ha-ha!' laughs Robin.

'Don't laugh at me!' the Sheriff cries. 'You'll be dead before the sun goes down this evening.'

'Can you kill me earlier, please?' Robin asks. 'I go to bed before the sun goes down. Ha-ha-ha!'

He runs up the stairs and looks down at the Sheriff.

'You're getting tired and I'm getting bored,' he tells the Sheriff.

'But you don't understand my new way of fighting,' answers the Sheriff. 'The robots are my teachers. Now I'm half man, half machine! You can't win!'

He follows Robin up the stairs and stands face to face with the younger man. 'You see. I don't get tired, and I'll never be old. You can't hurt me.'

The fight moves above the Sheriff's large bath of hot gold. Robin looks down at it. Is this the gold for the skyship?

'One day I *will* take England!' shouts the Sheriff.

'Why are you talking?' Robin asks. 'This is a fight!'

The Sheriff comes near Robin and cuts his arm with his sword. Robin's sword flies out of his hand and falls to the floor below him. What will Robin do without his sword? The Doctor and Clara watch and feel afraid for him.

'You're going to die now. Are you ready?' the Sheriff shouts at Robin.

Robin laughs again. The Sheriff tries to kill him with his sword. Robin is very angry now, but suddenly he remembers the Doctor's trick from the river. With his arms above his head, Robin turns quickly. He's now back to back with the Sheriff, and with a quick push he sends the older man into the sea of hot gold below.

The Doctor smiles happily. He knows that it was his trick. Clara also smiles at Robin, her hero.

With a quick push Robin sends the older man into the sea of hot gold below.

The Gold Arrow

Robin Hood runs quickly down the stairs.

'Did you enjoy that?' he cries. 'I did!'

'You were wonderful!' Clara tells him. 'I loved every minute!'

Suddenly something explodes in another room in the castle. The building is moving and walls are falling.

'The spaceship is starting to move! Run! Quickly!' the Doctor shouts at the two young people.

They run out of the castle and into the forest. At the same time, a gold hand comes out of the Sheriff's bath. Then it slowly goes down under the sea of hot gold again.

Smoke and fire follow the Doctor, Clara and Robin, but they get to the forest as quickly as possible. They meet the Merry Men there. Then they turn and watch. The castle falls and the spaceship flies into the sky.

'It's not going to work,' the Doctor tells everybody. 'Without more gold, it's going to explode. It's very, very dangerous. But wait! Where is it?'

'Where's what? What are you talking about?' Clara asks.

'The gold arrow. Quick! Somebody go and find it!' the Doctor shouts.

'Tuck! You had the gold arrow. Get it! Now!' Robin shouts.

Robin puts the gold arrow into the bow and pulls it back. Then the arrow flies into the sky. It hits the spaceship.

'*You* took it?' the Doctor asks.

'Of course we did. Remember? We take things from rich people,' Friar Tuck tells the Doctor. 'Here it is.'

'I love you boys!' the Doctor says.

'Doctor, do you have an idea? A plan?' Clara asks.

'Gold arrow. Gold!' the Doctor begins. 'We send this gold up to the spaceship. More gold won't repair the ship. But it will fly faster – and away from England – before it explodes.'

He gives the gold arrow to Robin.

'I'm sorry. I can't use my bow. Don't you remember?' Robin says sadly. 'The Sheriff cut my right arm. You'll have to do it, Doctor.'

The Doctor looks very unhappy with this idea.

'Doctor, you're very good with a bow and arrow,' Clara says. 'You're the best. We saw you at the contest. You were the winner!'

'But it was a trick. I made an arrow with a laser inside. It found the centre of the target without my help,' the Doctor tells everybody. 'Now what are we going to do?'

'Well, that's great!' Clara cries. 'Give *me* the bow and arrow. I'll try.'

'You don't know anything about bows and arrows,' the Doctor says.

'My friends,' Robin says to Clara and the Doctor. 'Three heads are better than one. Think!'

Clara, the Doctor and Robin sit on the ground. Then Clara and the Doctor each take one end of the bow in their hands.

'This has to work!' shouts the Doctor.

'Be quiet and help me,' Robin tells him.

Robin puts the gold arrow into the bow and pulls it back. Then the arrow flies into the sky. It hits the spaceship.

They hear a robot say, 'The spaceship is 100% ready.'

The spaceship suddenly goes much faster and higher into the sky. Everybody on the ground watches and waits.

The spaceship explodes. There is only a ball of fire in the sky.

'In Nottingham one fine day,
A skyship tried to fly away—'

  Will Scarlett puts a hand across Alan's mouth.

'Alan, it's not a good time for a song,' he says,
and everybody laughs.

'*Isn't* this a good time for a laugh, Doctor?' Clara asks.

'No, no, no! There's never a good time for laughing,' answers the Doctor.

He looks at Robin Hood and Clara. The Merry Men are watching them, too. Robin is teaching Clara about bows and arrows. She likes being near him.

'I'd like to stay in Sherwood Forest,' Clara says quietly to Robin. 'You're a wonderful man.'

Robin is teaching Clara about bows and arrows. She likes being near him.

'And you're lovely and very clever. And you always have good ideas and a lot of good tricks,' Robin says.

'Oh, I know,' Clara answers.

'You're a good woman,' says Robin.

'And your Marian knows that you're a good man,' Clara tells Robin.

'How can she know when she's away from me?' Robin says sadly. 'But perhaps she'll come home one day.'

'Always hope!' Clara tells him. 'She'll come home. And you? Be careful, but always be wonderful!'

'You're right! Ha-ha-ha!'

'Goodbye, Robin Hood.'

'Goodbye, Clara.'

Clara goes into the TARDIS. Before she closes the door, she sends a lovely smile back to Robin.

Robin turns to the Doctor.

'So, Doctor, what's my *real* story?' he asks.

'What do you mean?' the Doctor asks.

'In the future, what will people think of me? Will I be real – or will I be somebody from children's stories?' Robin asks.

'Well,' the Doctor begins, 'you'll only be a hero in storybooks. I'm sorry. Is that a problem?'

'Of course not,' Robin says. 'Real people have real problems. In stories, we can *fly*. We can go everywhere and do everything. Isn't that right?'

'I'll always have a problem with your story,' the Doctor answers.

'It's not difficult. Some men are born with a lot of money and a good name. But they see poor, sad people with problems. They look and they want to help,' Robin says.

'Hmm ...'

'And then they take the TARDIS.' Robin smiles. 'They fly into the sky and begin to fight for those poor, sad people. Clara told me your story. You're a *real* hero,' Robin tells the Doctor.

'I don't want her to tell my story,' the Doctor says.

'But your story's real, and you're Clara's hero,' Robin says.

'I'm *not* a hero,' the Doctor tells Robin.

'And *I'm* not! But we can try ... ha-ha-ha!' laughs Robin. 'Perhaps other people will learn about us and be heroes, too. Perhaps you and I will live in stories for hundreds and hundreds of years.'

'Perhaps. Goodbye, Robin of Loxley.'

'Goodbye, Doctor. And remember – I'm as real as you are.'

'Robin! I found you!'
the young woman cries.

The Doctor smiles and walks into the TARDIS. He and Clara turn on the time machine and put into the computer: *England. London. About the year 2018.*

'You began to like him,' Clara says to the Doctor with a smile.

'Well, he tells a good story. And I'm leaving something for him. Look down into Sherwood Forest.'

Clara looks down and sees Robin with a young woman. She is the Doctor's companion from the dungeon, the young woman from the small house near the forest.

'Robin! I found you!' the young woman cries.

'Marian? Marian! Is it really you? Ha-ha-ha!' Robin laughs happily.

The TARDIS flies past and Robin looks up.

'Thank you. Thank you, Doctor!' he cries. 'You're my hero!'

Activities

Chapters 1-2

Before you read

1 Look at the Word List at the back of the book. Then discuss these questions.

a Can you name three *heroes* from film or television?

b Can you name a story with a *castle* and a *dungeon* in it?

c How are the lives of *poor* people and rich people different in your country?

d Do you plays *tricks* on other people? What was your best trick?

e Can you name:

 - three *machines* in your kitchen?
 - another use for a *laser*?
 - three jobs for *robots*?
 - three things in a *forest*?

2 What do you know about these people?

the Doctor   Robin Hood

Talk about them. Then read about them – and the other people in this story – in In this story, at the beginning of the book.

3 Now read the Introduction to this book and answer these questions.

a In what year does this story happen?

b In which place?

c Who wants to meet Robin Hood?

d How will the Doctor and his companion make the journey?

While you read

4 Circle the correct words in these sentences.

a The TARDIS moves *quickly* / *slowly* from one place and time to another.

b Robin Hood lives in *the TARDIS / Sherwood Forest*.

c The Doctor uses a *sword / spoon* in his fights.

d The Doctor wins most of his fights because he is *old / clever*.

e The Doctor falls into the river because of *an accident / a trick*.

f Robin Hood loves *Marian / the Sheriff*.

g The Sheriff of Nottingham lives in a *castle / small house*.

h England usually has green trees and warm weather in the *summer / autumn*.

i Robin Hood uses a *gun / bow and arrow* in the contest.

j Mr Quayle *lives / dies* when the Sheriff visits.

k The Sheriff *wins / loses* the contest.

l The Sheriff's knights are *men / robots*.

m *The Doctor doesn't want / wants* to go into the castle.

After you read

5 Discuss these questions with another student. Why ...

a does the Doctor have a problem with a journey to Sherwood Forest?

b are the Merry Men important to Robin Hood?

c does the Doctor look carefully at the Merry Men when he meets them?

d aren't the Sheriff of Nottingham and Robin Hood friends?

e does Clara think that the contest for the gold arrow is a trick?

f does Mr Quayle die?

g is Robin Hood angry with the Doctor after the contest for the gold arrow?

h is Clara angry with the Doctor and Robin in the dungeon?

Chapters 3-4

Before you read

6 You are one of these people. Tell the class about your feelings.

a You are the Doctor. How do you feel about
   Clara?   Robin Hood?

b You are Robin Hood. How do you feel about
   the Sheriff?   the Merry Men?   Clara?

c You are Clara. How do you feel about
the Doctor?   Robin Hood?

d You are the Sheriff. How do you feel about
Robin Hood?   Mr Quayle?   the Doctor?

While you read

7   Who is speaking? Who are they talking to? Where are they?

a 'But tonight we'll sleep. Then we can help Robin in the morning.'

b 'More beautiful plates!'

c 'I'm only a poor, weak girl. A strong, clever man always speaks first.'

d 'My friend's very ill. He always feels ill when he's afraid.'

e 'Nobody in Nottingham in 1190 was as well and as strong as you. Tell me your robot name.'

f 'We're going to live – not die!'

After you read

8   Why are these important? Discuss them with another student.

a the Sheriff's bags of gold
b the Sheriff's large bath
c the Doctor's sonic screwdriver
d the problem with the robots' spaceship
e pictures of Robin Hood from storybooks and films
f two explosions in the spaceship

Chapters 5-6

Before you read

9 Work with a friend. Have this conversation.

Student A: You are Clara. Tell the Doctor about your conversation with the Sheriff in his dining-room. What did you learn? Answer the Doctor's questions. Then ask about his story.

Student B: You are the Doctor. Listen to Clara's story and ask questions. Then tell Clara about the computers in the spaceship. What did you learn? Answer her questions.

While you read

10 Write the names. Who ...

   a tells the story of the Doctor?   ....
   b wants to go to London in the spaceship?   ....
   c helps the Doctor in his fight with the
   robot-knights in the dungeon?   ....
   d explodes when a laser hits them?   ....
   e now understands that the Sheriff and
   Robin Hood are *not* friends?   ....
   f laughs at the Sheriff when they fight?   ....
   g dies in the sea of hot gold?   ....

After you read

11 Finish these sentences. Then show your answers to another student. Do you have different ideas?

   a Clara enjoys her time in Sherwood Forest because ...
   b The young woman from Mr Quayle's house wants to help the Doctor because ...
   c Many robots die in the dungeon because ...
   d The Sheriff is excited when he looks at a map of the world because ...
   e The spaceship is dangerous because ...
   f Robin is important to the people of Nottingham because ...
   g Robin wins his fight with the Sheriff because ...

Chapter 7

Before you read

12 **What is going to happen next? Discuss your answers.**

    a Are Robin Hood and the Doctor going to be friends?
    b Is the young woman from the dungeon going to come into the story again?
    c What is going to happen to the spaceship?
    d Will the Doctor and Clara stay in Sherwood Forest for a long time?

While you read

13 **Are these sentences right (✔) or wrong (✘)?**

    a The Sheriff dies in the sea of hot gold.
    b Friar Tuck took the gold arrow on the day of the contest.
    c The Doctor and Clara are good with a bow and arrow.
    d The spaceship kills half the people in England.
    e The Merry Men ask Alan-a-Dale to sing another song.
    f Robin wants Marian to come back to Sherwood Forest one day.
    g Marian goes to London with the Doctor and Clara.

After you read

14 **Who do you think has these ideas in their head? Why?**

    a 'These Merry Men are more intelligent than I thought.'
    b 'I can't hit the skyship with my bow and the gold arrow without two good arms.
    c 'Now I have two heroes!'
    d 'Sherwood Forest was interesting, but next time we'll go to a real place.'
    e 'Marian came back! My future looks good.'
    f 'I don't laugh much, but I'm happy with the end of this story.'

Writing

15 Many things happened to Marian and to Robin Hood when Marian was away. Write a conversation between them on Marian's first day back in Sherwood Forest.

16 Write a newspaper story about the end of the Sheriff of Nottingham.

17 You are Alan-a-Dale. Write the words to a song about the Doctor and Clara's visit to Sherwood Forest.

18 You are Clara. You like the Doctor, Robin Hood and the Merry Men. You don't like The Sheriff of Nottingham. Write a letter to your best friend about men. What do you think makes a good man or a bad man?

19 Write a newspaper story about Nottingham's greatest hero, Robin Hood.

20 Clara wants to visit another hero from a storybook. The Doctor wants to visit a real person in a real place. Write the conversation between them.

21 You are an important person and have a beautiful dining-room in your castle. Write an invitation and a menu for a wonderful dinner for eight important visitors.

22 You have a time machine for one month. Where do you want to go? In what year? Who do you want to meet?

Word List

bow and arrow (n phr) In the days before guns, people in many countries killed people and animals with *bows and arrows*.

castle (n) The important, rich people in old stories usually lived in big, beautiful *castles*.

contest (n) The last *contest* was between the six fastest swimmers.

dungeon (n) She killed my brother. Take her underground to the dark, wet *dungeon* and leave her there.

explode (v) When the plane hit the ground, it *exploded*. We heard the *explosion* from a long way away.

forest (n) You can find a lot of different trees in a British *forest*.

gold (n) After twenty-five years with the company, her boss gave her a *gold* watch.

hero (n) Superman, Batman, Wonder Woman and Iron Man are *heroes* in books and films.

knight (n) *Knights* were fighters. In stories, they also helped other people.

laser (n) The doctor used a *laser* on my eye and now I can see better.

machine (n) Our washing *machines*, our cars and many other machines help us every day.

poor (adj) *Poor* people have to work hard for food and for their homes.

radiation (n) When a lot of *radiation* comes from some machines, it can be dangerous to people and to the world.

real (adj) Harry Potter is very famous, but he isn't *real*.

repair (n/v) We can't drive anywhere. The garage is making *repairs* to our car.

robot (n) One day *robots* will clean our houses and cook our food.

space (n) Yuri Gagarin, a Russian, was the first person in *space*. He flew round the Earth in a Vostok **spaceship**.

sword (n) She fought with a *sword* and cut the other woman's leg.

target (n) He carries a gun, but he can't hit a *target* in the garden.

trick (n) People like clever card *tricks* because they can't understand them.

BBC

DOCTOR WHO

Who is Doctor Who?

Meet the Doctor, a 2000–year–old Time Lord and an unconventional hero. Together with his companion, Clara Oswald, he travels through space and time, often saving the day.

All *Doctor Who* Readers
are available as

📖 Print Book
📖 Print Book with Audio CD
🎧 eBook with integrated audio

Teacher resources
are available to download from
www.pearsonenglishreaders.com

Based on the BBC series *Doctor Who*, the longest running sci-fi and family drama in the world, Pearson English Readers bring you a new series of extraordinary adventures!

Pearson English **Readers**

Robot of Sherwood

A story based on the original script by Mark Gatiss

Pearson English **Readers**

Flatline

A story based on the original script by Jamie Mathieson

Pearson English **Readers**

Mummy on the Orient Express

A story based on the original script by Jamie Mathieson

Pearson English **Readers**

The Girl Who Died

A story based on the original script by Jamie Mathieson

Pearson English **Readers**

Face the Raven

A story based on the original script by Sarah Dollard

Pearson English **Readers**

The Woman Who Lived

A story based on the original script by Catherine Tregenna

Pearson English **Readers**

BBC